Is it possible to weave the tapestry of Life

While unraveling the threads of mystery?

~ Lorenzo Cherubini

Also by Lorenzo Cherubini

Some Words and Thoughts, Somewhat of a Rap, and the Parasitic Gap

Situating Thinking and Reflection: Studying Teaching and Learning

Case Study Inquiry Seminars: A Research-to-Practice Model (2nd Edition)

Aboriginal Student Engagement and Achievement: Educational Practices and Cultural Sustainability.

Case-Study Inquiry Seminars: A Research to Practice Model

That Space Which is Thinking: Prospective Teacher Identity

Re-searching the Historical Present: Implications on Aboriginal Education, Policy and Schools

Standardized Assessment and Classroom Evaluation: A Comprehensive Examination

Projecting Self and Actualizing Teaching: Prospective Teacher Consciousness

The Study of Identity as a Concept and Social Construct in Behavioral and Social Science Research: Interdisciplinary and Global Perspectives.

An Ideology of Crisis and Identity: Learning about 'Life under the Rocks of the Tide Pool.'

Reflections and Perceptions, a Touch of Euphoria, and a Reprieve from Misophonia

Lorenzo Cherubini

720 Sixth Street, Unit #5
New Westminster, BC
V3L 3C5
CANADA

Title: Reflections and Perceptions, a Touch of Euphoria
        and a Reprieve from Misophonia
Author: Lorenzo Cherubini
Publisher: Silver Bow Publishing
Cover Art: "Kewpie Doll Flowers"
            painting by Candice James
Layout/Design: Candice James
Editing: Candice James

All rights reserved including the right to reproduce or translate this book or any portions thereof, in any form without the permission of the publisher. Except for the use of short passages for review purposes, no part of this book may be reproduced, in part or in whole, or transmitted in any form or by any means, either by means electronically or mechanically, including photocopying, recording, or any information or storage retrieval system without prior permission in writing from the publisher or a licence from the Canadian Copyright Collective Agency (Access Copyright).

www.silverbowpublishing.com
info@silverbowpublishing.com
ISBN: 978-1-77403-108-7 paperback
ISBN: 978-1-77403-109-4 electronic book
© Silver Bow Publishing

Library and Archives Canada Cataloguing in Publication

Title: Reflections and perceptions, a touch of euphoria, and a reprieve from misophonia / by
   Lorenzo Cherubini.
Names: Cherubini, Lorenzo, author.
Description: Poems.
Identifiers: Canadiana (print) 20200254383 | Canadiana (ebook) 20200254405 | ISBN 9781774031087
    (softcover) | ISBN 9781774031094 (EPUB)
Classification: LCC PS8605.H466 R44 2020 | DDC C811/.6—dc23

To what is beyond reason ...

and logic.

With thanks to Candice James,

for sharing the poetry of her portraits.

Preface

Life is circumstantial.
Entails central impulses.
Evokes and problematizes emotion.
Offers certitudes and doubts.
But always embedded in relations.
This collection of poetry is an introspection.
Of varied perceptions
that implicate living.
Some euphoric.
Others more despondent.
Though ...
All the poems offer a sense of reprieve
even if only momentary.
From the turmoil.
The unrest.
And the confusion ...
That prevails in the delicate depths of your being.
That only you can understand
Since it is only yours to endure.

First Lines of Poems

To function fully in Being ... 13
When carefully crafted ... 14
The behaviour falls within the broad spectrum ... 15
People inhabit the world ... 16
To have once been competent ... 17
A felt inaptness ... 18
The domestication of anger ... 19
Publicizing success ... 20
Interpretation and perception ... 21
What should be considered ... 22
Impinging disruptively on stability ... 23
To fuel the controversy of decorum ... 24
It is implication-less ... 25
The fearless determination to be you ... 26
Being forced to witness ... 27
Greed – a historical actor ... 28
A testimony to your Being ... 29
Being within the gaze of the one that creates ... 30
It has always been like that ... 31
Tolerating ignorance ... 32
Living bereft of Will ... 33
Examining assumptions ... 34
A false idea ... 35
Inviting transparency ... 36
Fractured selves ... 37
Tumultuous relations ... 38
Lacking awareness ... 39.
What makes the Other invisible ... 40
Neglecting history ... 41
It is beyond all that is merely conditioned ... 42
Establishing policy ... 43
Do you imagine it? ... 44
Cannot separate the behaviour ... 45
The reality of cultural influence ... 46

To conform to the collective ... 47
The development of certain tendencies ... 48
An outcome of imprudent discretion ... 49
To live with inextinguishable hope ... 50
Inserting a difference to view it differently ... 51
It must all appear so strange ... 52
Our activity is beholden to those that came before ... 53
Where is the sphere of existential confusion...? ... 54
Searching for the locality of your belief ... 55
Societal expectations to regulate ... 56
To quell the tempest of confusion ... 57
The discreteness of our existence ... 58
In the aversion of risk ... 59
A climate of cultural ownership ... 60
Is there a possibility to counter-memory? ... 61
A modest engagement with the Creator ... 62
Moderation and pace ... 63
Duality and conflict ... 64
The tendencies of erosion not exclusive to rock and ... 65
To be in harmony and solidarity ... 66
The cradle of hate ... 67
Is it natural to elicit empathy? ... 68
Were you once a previous incarnation of someone else? .69
How will we know ... 70
Do we tend to be cynical in our views ...? ... 71
Times of confounding dissention ... 72.
The outcome is to be non-lonely ... 73.
Human response to suffering ... 74
What is the mark of distinction? ... 75
Feeling uneasy in the social margins ... 76
To whom does one appeal? ... 77
Don't be fooled by Persona ... 78
There are those said to be impermeable ... 79
Transitioning into one's destiny ... 80
An unanticipated spiritual discovery ... 81.

The spirit can mediate truth … 82.
Is aspiration the property of only a few? … 83
Welcoming contests and conflict … 84
Those who re-side with less … 85
Reflection as all-pervasive … 86.
Is there a direct response to presumption? … 87
To be indebted to another … 88
The invisible scaffold of passing Time … 89
Requiring and inviting elusiveness … 90
Is it possible to weave the tapestry of Life … 91
Daily existence … 92
When the brushstrokes of Life transform … 93
Un-settle-ness is convincingly worrying … 94
What is your life's composition? … 95
It is an ancient art … 96
A matter of moral indignation … 97
The commission to be of faith …98
To hold on to the images that once were … 99
To exist in indecision … 100
Is it possible to be impartial … 101
Lingering in consciousness … 102
We are a fragile species … 103
What is your Route 66? … 104
It is a bitter irony of life … 105
Such a profound gap between generations … 106
Taking refuge in jealousy … 107.
Impulsive actions and desires … 108
To come-of-age … 109
Is there prudence to the paradoxes? … 110

Author Profile … 111

To function fully in Being.
To access meaningful enactment.
To approach the sanctioned spaces of relations.
And cross multiple scopes of appearance.
And perception.
To engage in pluralistic views.

When carefully crafted,
What defines beauty?
A mere contestable idea that houses universal perception?
A notion married to sensitivity and indebted to the few?
Is beauty a function of cognition?
Or perhaps a habit of reason?

Is it sufficiently powerful to recast differently?
Resilient to the vipers of critique
when carefully crafted?
What defines beauty?

The behaviour falls within the broad spectrum.
Of that condition.
There is memory loss.
Abandonment of short-term recollection.
The mind's wrath on your senses.
Awkwardness is obvious.
Dis-jointed annotations.
A mutual heartbreak of mortal existence.

People inhabit the world.
Shared experiences.
Marked in different ways.
Often a sense of the familiar in the ebb and flow.
Often responses to both the common and absurd.

To have once been competent.
Overly-so.
Sensitive to the invisible needs of others.
Attentive to their silent requests.
To have once personified connection.
A charisma with a deliberate purpose.
It's all changing.
Feeling the gradual granular release
of my senses through
the gritty fingertips
of normality.
Difficult to focus.
And to remember.
Living merely descriptively.

A felt inaptness.
Self – and other-threatening.
Drifting in the existential.
Introspectively incongruent.
Conditioned hyper-realities.
A felt inaptness.

The domestication of anger.
A civil action.
Civic requirement.
But counter-evolutionary?
Counter-revolutionary?
Behavioural expression
or
Genetic repression?
The domestication of anger.
Conducted in public.
Experienced in secret.
A proper understanding of these effects?
No obvious causations.
Violent functionalities of cross-historical models.
Requires conversation.
But only in a dialogue of tolerance.

Publicizing success.
Appealing to faces of wished engagement.
Broadcasting ambition.
According to self-promotion.
Pervading impact upon others.

Interpretation and perception.
Subject to the senses.
Mutually reinforcing.
The core elements that are the gateway to understanding.

What should be considered
against the backdrop of believing?
Amidst the spectrum of divine truths?
Across the realms of wonder?
...
Perhaps only the imperative to illuminate meaning.

Impinging disruptively on stability.
Piercing intimate spaces.
Shattering private symmetry.
Confusing all that is ...
Chiselling away at patience.
The pangs of misophonia.
A disruptive cadence.

To fuel the controversy of decorum.
A flurry of social forces.
And expectations.
Not for lack of etiquette.
The silent virtues of publicly accepted behaviour.
Suppressing orientations to the primal...
To interwoven desires masked
by the superficiality of decorum.

It is implication-less.
A tendency to surface unexpectedly.
Invites a collision with Other-ness.
A misunderstanding of how to function.
Yet
is a human pattern.
A tendency to uncloak coarseness.
A glaring darkness in the absence of light.

The fearless determination to be you.
An eccentric biography
Of
Endurance
Courage
And
Determination.
Neither written in the stars
Nor cast in stone.
Just a fame and fortune,
Of you alone.

Being forced to witness
The spectacle of Hemingway's Pamplona.
The blood and gore of the ring.
A re-enactment of all that is primal.

Greed – a historical actor.
In and of its own.
Defiant in its cause.
A propensity towards dominance.
Includes nuanced understandings of the exclusionary self.
A racialized presence in the collective.

A testimony to your Being.
An articulation of observation.
A sharing in the collective.
Stunning episodes.
Epic influence.
A testimony to your Being,
Your sense of difference across channels.

Being within the gaze of the one that creates.
Generates numerous images.
And peers into the un-known.
Being within the gaze of the one that creates.
Privately mediated.
And delving into the expansive.

It has always been like that.
Surely you know.
Possibly related to selfish-ness?
Possibly self-centred-ness?
It has always been like that.
A mere juxtaposition of irony.
Emanating from envy.
It has always been like that.

Tolerating ignorance.
Broadly defined.
Broadly (mis)understood.

Living bereft of Will.
An extinguished flame.
A burned candle.

Examining assumptions.
Interwoven beliefs.
Deliberate concepts of popularity.
An interrogation of neutrality.

A false idea.
Irrelevance abounds.
Socially worrisome.
An appeal to chaos.

Inviting transparency.
Accounting for protocol.
And regulation.
Even management.
Seeking order and process.
Having the courage to proceed.

Fractured selves.
Shattering.
Terrifying.
Residually fear-full.
Severed from Other.
Fractured selves.
Disheartened ambition.
Shaken.
To the core.
Fractured selves.

Tumultuous relations.
Struggle for understanding.
Somber glances of disdain.
Locked into the narrative of hate.

Lacking awareness.
Clouded by self-doubt.
Mechanical behaviour.
Barely.
Existing in space-less-ness.
A profound confusion of will.

What makes the Other invisible?
Tendency to ignore?
Evaporating priorities?
Relative apathy?
Apathetic relativity?
Or just a convenient indiscernibility?

Neglecting history.
Ignoring the crusades.
Recognizing
But not comprehending.
Representing
But not contemplating.

It is beyond all that is merely conditioned.
Has to be.
It is subsumed into consciousness.
Perhaps elsewhere.
A familiar stranger waiting to be (re)introduced.
Their visage a transcendental appearance.

Establishing policy.
Complicated, but necessary.
Determined political actions...
And official proclamations.
Immersed in the obscure web of relations...
That sometimes silence.

Do you imagine it?
At times from different locations?
Is there a voice that echoes…?
that tells?
Do you speculate what could be?
Imagine it?
Even if it generates distress?
Is there noise in Faulkner's sound?
And ferocity in his fury?

Cannot separate the behaviour
From you.
Can rationalize the difference,
But cannot reason with its effect.
Can distill love,
But cannot connect with like.
It is minutiae for others,
But distressing for me.

The reality of cultural influence.
The totality of neutralized relations.
The function of the interplay.
The purpose of tradition.

To conform to the collective
and sustain harmonious ways.
To infer agreeability,
and avoid alienation.
To approach the dialogue meekly,
and avert all that might be contentious.

The development of certain tendencies.
Circumstantial and contextual.
Necessary to swim down-stream
and become complex visions of our-selves.
The development of certain tendencies.
Temporally meaningful.
Implicit to social literacy.
Conscious design and action.
Possibly biologically driven...?

An outcome of imprudent discretion?
A disregard for custom?
Biased judgements...
An appalling path towards indifference.

To live with inextinguishable hope.
And suspend contingency to pursue all that is possible.

Inserting a difference to view it differently.
Honouring what is relative.
Knowing it is all relative.
Foremost relative.
Futile to presume...
to eclipse the light of relativity.
And to allude the ensuing relevance of it all.

It must all appear so strange.
Tragically sur-real.
Not remembering yesterday ... sometimes not even today.
Sudden and emotional tangents
Unhinged from once-safe harbours.
Grappling with exceptionally useless detail.
Looking for consolation in the sublime
And terrifying engagements.

Our activity is beholden to those that came before.
Those who brought order to the concept of our Truth.

Where is the sphere of existential confusion amongst us?
Woven in our movement...
Embodied in our thought...
Swirling in the storm of our present.

Searching for the locality of your belief.
Not an inconsequential endeavor.
Affords a compelling examination of what rests in-side.
Yields the fragility of the most intimate communion.

Societal expectations to regulate.
Emotion.
Empathy.
Feeling.
The imperative to serve functionality
And stabilize expectation.

To quell the tempest of confusion
and the turbulence of doubt.
To recall the origins of self
and seek shelter from the gusts of criticism.

The discreteness of our existence.
A mosaic of perceptions...
Commanded by responses.
Draws upon all eventualities.
A complex infusion of our interior self.

In the aversion of risk
lies the underlying assumption
of resignation.

A climate of cultural ownership.
Politically controversial.
Socially un-becoming.
Perilously close to insult.
What is the challenge?
And the response?
To summon the courage of genuine inquiry.

Is there a possibility to counter-memory?
A re-investigation of the chronicles of oppression?
Not, though, to explain.
Neither to rationalize.
That is not for us.
But instead,
to be preoccupied with truth...
With order...
With sense...
With meaning-making.

A modest engagement with the Creator.
Necessary if only to stabilize the perplexity...
the dumbfounded-ness.
And aspire for the liberty to believe.

Moderation and pace.
In nature.
Across seasons and cycles.
Uncompromising routine.
An orchestra of order.

Duality and conflict.
Self-propelling gears.
The machinery that has been engineered.

The tendencies of erosion – not exclusive to rock and stone.
Decay of vitality – not exclusive to the weak and elderly.
Compression of experience – the marble of our lives.

To be in harmony and solidarity.
Aligned with the symbolic order of all that was.
To unveil the obscurity of the mystery.
And emerge from the viability of all that is.

The cradle of hate.
Rest-less jealousy.
Tranquility haunted by ineptness.

Is it natural to elicit empathy?
And be deliberate on the exchange of cruelty and kindness?
Is it acceptable to readily concede emotion?
And mark a range of experiential feeling?

Were you once a previous incarnation of someone else?
Of something else?
Were you born from the realm of another?
Did you emerge with a new purpose?
Are you simply re-seeded in a different captive space?

How will we know,
if the bonds of civility are severed?

Do we tend to be cynical in our views ...?
Even of what is important?

Times of confounding dissention.
An onus to dis-rupt harmony.
A medley of existing and proposed perspectives.
No tolerance for not-Us.
Yet ...
Inability to distinguish the immediate meaning.
If there is one.

The outcome is to be non-lonely.
And to be non-confrontational.
To adopt a non-critical disposition.
And to be non-dis-engaged.
You can-not be forthright.
You can-not be judicious.
Dare not invite indifference and
welcome candour.

Human response to suffering.
Viewed as legitimate.
The beginnings of withdrawn-ness.
Courting anguish.
Beckoning pain.

What is the mark of distinction?
How does its enactment make it significantly better?
Where are the ancestral roots of honour?
Does it exist at the crossroads of class consciousness?

Feeling uneasy in the social margins.
Awkward in politically contested spaces.
Balancing the contrast
that is us.
Convoluted identities across the social parade.
Discourses of transgression.
Pitiful to reflect same-ness.
A not-so-simple juxtaposition of individual Selves.

To whom does one appeal?
When the interior fails?
When the sense of coherence is in dis-array?
Memories in denial.
Stories lodged in private spaces.
Inaccessible places.
A dullened mind of elusive understandings.
And we left helplessly ...
At the gates of misery.

Don't be fooled by Persona.
Neither yours nor theirs.
It is a mere obscurity to terrifying realization.
If it is unleashed.
From within.
Better to illuminate the boundaries of our Being,
Than to compromise sanity by un-masking the multiplicity of our desire.

There are those said to be impermeable.
Resistant to feeling.
Suspicious of emotion.
Hard.
Impossible to engage.
Closed.
Intensively evasive.
Cold.
Embodies a counter-Aristotelian dependence.

Transitioning into one's destiny.
Staring into blankness.
Flickering shadows of doubt.
Implied across multiple dimensions.
Articulations of (mere) possibility.
Inconclusive tomorrows.
Transition influx –
What else could it be?

An unanticipated spiritual discovery.
An impetus to perceive – differently.
Sensing grandeur.
An expansion of the sixth sense.
A euphoric glimpse of tranquility.
An unanticipated spiritual discovery.

The spirit can mediate truth.
It can be insipid.
In its ambition.
And force.
The spirit can mediate truth.
It can be authentic.
In its reflection to Self.
It can manifest in a secret dialogue.
The spirit can mediate truth.

Is aspiration the property of only a few?
Solely the privileged?
Are there relations of ownership to be negotiated?
Or merely inherited by the fortunate?
The rhetoric of aspiration is not of the common dialogue.
A commodity often bestowed ...
And denied ...
By the ambitious.

Welcoming contests and conflict.
Immersed in community.
Literal and storied depictions.
Flashing images of compromised ideals.
Parlaying encounters in time and place.

Those who re-side with less.
Experience the tangibility of poverty.
Material struggle.
Targets of discernment.
Shrewdness.
Concede to isolation.
Always on the outside looking in.

Reflection as all-pervasive.
Open-minded-ness to points of arrival.
Time-less thoughts ...
About ...
The inevitability of Significance.

Is there a direct response to presumption?
Perceptible instances of predictability?
Surely there is more than sheer random-ness,
in the inferences that matter.

To be indebted to another.
To their self-less spirit and cause.
To the human dimensions that leverage difference.
To their integral composition.

The invisible scaffold of passing Time.
Momentary experiences of pertinence.
Suggestive of aspirations ...
That there is something more.

Requiring and inviting elusiveness.
Calling for a profound understanding of essence.
Coping in in-between-ness.
But depending upon grounded identities.

Is it possible to weave the tapestry of Life,
While unraveling the threads of mystery?

Daily existence.
Merely routine.
Predictable patterns.
The sentinel of Order.
A fascinating collection of habits.

When the brushstrokes of Life transform.
Lose colour and tint.
Abandon, affect.
When perception is shaded by
black and white.
And the marvel of colour surrenders to only what is.

Episodes of expression-less encounters.
Slipping from the foothold of meaning.
And satisfaction.
Forgetting to rewind time
and lavish in memories.
Remembering to not stare into the eyes of tomorrow
to manage the conviction-less moment.

What is your life's composition?
What are the circumstances that have led to its creation?
The notes that have breathed harmony
into your movements?
The melodies of your classical style?
What is your life's composition?

It is an ancient art.
Perceiving
and feeling all that is extant.
In the moment.
Appealing to sharpness.
Liberating breath.
Natural gestures.

A matter of moral indignation.
No explanatory devices.
Desperate frames of reference.
Suspends us in liminal spaces.
Unnerving encounters even with ourselves.

The commission to be of faith.
Incentives to...
Aspire to something greater.
Someone greater.
Beyond proportion and public gaze.
Empirically transcendent.
Yet ...
Resonates across the essence of Being.

To hold on to the images that once were.
To sketch the visions with black accents
and border the days gone by.
The apprenticeship of loss
blotched on the palette of recollections.

To exist in indecision.
Is to challenge the paradigms of certainty,
And to contemplate
Provisions of how certitudes change.

Is it possible to be impartial
to the subjective experiences
of our lives?

Lingering in consciousness.
Un-forgettable experiences.
Un-mistakable impressions.
Re-markable imprints.
Yet extra-ordinarily private.
Its impact confined to the property of self.

We are a fragile species
Of coincidental relations.

What is your Route 66?
Steinbeck's dust.
Your hardship and sacrifice.
Your strained ties.
What have you lost?
What hearts have been closed?
Surely this has been part of your travel …
What is your evocation of humanity's good?

It is a bitter irony of life.
Demoralizing effects on the Other.
Seemingly spiteful habits that
Though not physically taxing,
Are emotionally grating.
You must know?
You must know.
You must know what it is doing to me?

Such a profound gap between generations.
The immigrants that came before.
Blended into the tapestry of the West.
Foreign language and customs.
Diverse traditions.
Sacrifice and tribulation, the necessary complexities of merging successfully.
Closing the gap between generations.

Taking refuge in jealousy.
Justifying envy to satisfy ego.
Charting suspicion to reason with wants.
Marshalling animosity as the soldiers of your cause.

Impulsive actions and desires.
Shunning self-consciousness.
For immediate gratification.

To come-of-age.
Cogently.
And assume a distinct place.
Position.
A fusing of core values.
Definitively.
Perceiving from outward eyes.
Intensely.
To come-of-age.

Is there prudence to the paradoxes?
Truth in false romanticism?
Deception in common convention?
Is there prudence to the paradoxes?
Duplicity in what is regimented?
Autonomy in the suppression of thought?
There is prudence to the paradoxes.

Author Profile:

Lorenzo Cherubini is a Professor at Brock University, St. Catharines, Ontario, Canada. His research is concentrated primarily in the areas of Indigenous education (policy) and critical literacy and is funded by the Social Science and Humanities Research Council of Canada (SSHRC).

He has published more than 100 refereed articles and proceedings, authored eight book chapters, and written nine books. He has also presented more than 80 refereed conference papers across Canada, the United States, Europe, South America, Asia, Africa and Oceania.

He was the recipient of the 2014 McGraw Hill Distinguished Scholar Award presented at the 26th *Annual Ethnographic and Qualitative Research* and the 17th *Annual American Association of Behavioral and Social Sciences Conferences* in Nevada and he is the former Editor of the *AABSS Journal* - an annual publication of the American Association of Behavioral and Social Sciences (AABSS).

He earned an Ed.D. from the University of Southern Queensland, Toowoomba, Australia and an M.A. at McMaster University, Hamilton, Ontario, Canada.

ALSO BY LORENO CHERUBINI

Books

Cherubini, L. (2017). *Situating Thinking and Reflection: Studying Teaching and Learning*. Welland, ON: Soleil Publishing. ISBN: 978-894935-98-2.

Cherubini, L. (2017). *Case Study Inquiry Seminars: A Research-to-Practice Model*. (Second Edition). Welland, ON: Soleil Publishing. ISBN: 978-1-894935-97-5.

Cherubini, L. (2014). *Aboriginal Student Engagement and Achievement: Educational Practices and Cultural Sustainability*. Vancouver, British Columbia: UBC Press. ISBN: 978-0-7748-2655-6.

Cherubini, L. (2013). *Case-Study Inquiry Seminars: A Research to Practice Model*. Welland, ON: Soleil Publishing. ISBN 978-1-894935-71-5

Cherubini, L. (2013). *That Space Which is Thinking: Prospective Teacher Identity*. Welland, ON: Soleil Publishing. ISBN 978-1-894935-73-9

Cherubini, L. (2012). *Re-searching the Historical Present: Implications on Aboriginal Education, Policy and Schools*. Saarbruken, Germany: Lambert Academic Publishing. ISBN 978-3-8473-4592-3

Cherubini, L. (2012). *Standardized Assessment and Classroom Evaluation: A Comprehensive Examination*. Saarbruken, Germany: Lambert Academic Publishing. ISBN 978-3-8473-4650-0

Cherubini, L. (2011). *Projecting Self and Actualizing Teaching: Prospective Teacher Consciousness*. Welland, ON: Soleil Publishing. ISBN: 978-1894935586

Cherubini, L. (Ed.). (2010). *The Study of Identity as a Concept and Social Construct in Behavioral and Social Science Research: Interdisciplinary and Global Perspectives*. Lewiston, New York: Mellen Press. ISBN-13: 978-0-7734-1452-5 & ISBN-10: 0-7734-1452-5

Cherubini, L. (1993; 2011). *An Ideology of Crisis and Identity: Learning about 'Life under the Rocks of the Tide Pool.'* Saarbruken, Germany: Lambert Academic Publishing. ISBN: 978-3-8443-9168-8.

Edited Textbook Publications

Cherubini, L. (Ed.). (2010). *Teaching, Learning and Schooling: A Reflective Engagement*. Toronto, ON: Pearson Publishing. ISBN: 9780558711795

Cherubini, L. (Ed.). (2006). *Contextualizing Pedagogical Practice: A Critical Awareness.* Toronto, ON: Pearson Publishing. ISBN: 0536296766

Book Chapters

Cherubini, L. (2014). "Indigenous groups' education: The case of North America" In. C. Brock & R. Griffin (Eds.), *Education in Indigenous, Nomadic and Travelling Communities* (pp. 149-168). London: Bloomsbury Press.

Cherubini, L. (2014). "Commentary: Experiencing a shared space for dialogue with First Nations community members." In D. Smith (Ed.), *A Call to Vocation: Narratives of Catholic Educators*. Toronto, ON: Pearson, pp.44-46.

Cherubini, L. (2011). "Breaking the mold to mend the wounds: An innovative model of collaborative practice to further Aboriginal student learning." In A. Cohan & A. Honigsfeld (Eds.), Breaking the Mold of Preservice and Inservice Teacher Education: Innovative and Successful Practices for the Twenty-first Century. New York: Rowman & Littlefield, pp. 259-268.

Cherubini, L., & Hodson, J. (2011). "Heightening awareness and strengthening relationships: Implications of public policy for Aboriginal students, communities and teachers." In J. Reyhner, W.S. Gilbert & L. Lockard (Eds.), Honoring our Heritage: Culturally Appropriate Approaches for Teaching Indigenous Students. Flagstaff, Arizona: Northern Arizona University Press, pp.173-195.

Cherubini, L. (2010). "(Re) Imagining identity: A Large Scale Case Study of Prospective Teachers' Perceptions." In L. Cherubini (Ed.), *The Study of Identity as a Concept and Social Construct in Behavioral and Social Science Research: Inter-Disciplinary and Global Perspectives*. Mellen Press. ISBN: 0773414525.

Cherubini, L., & Hodson, J. (2010). "Aboriginal Educational Policy and Practice in Ontario Public Schools: Implications on Student and

Teacher Identity." In L. Cherubini (Ed.), *The Study of Identity as a Concept and Social Construct in Behavioral and Social Science Research: Inter-Disciplinary and Global Perspectives*. Mellen Press. ISBN: 0773414525.

Cherubini, L., & Volante, L. (2010). "Policies and paradox: A view of school leadership in the context of Aboriginal education in Ontario, Canada." In A. Normore (Ed.), *Global Perspectves on Educational Leadership Reform: The Development and Preparation of Leaders of Learning and Learners of Leadership,* Volume 11. Emerald Press, pp. 125-141.

Cherubini, L. (2006). "Impressions of fabricated discernment: A discourse analysis of beginning teachers." In M. Firmin & P. Brewer (Eds.), *Ethnographic and Qualitative Research in Education*, Vol II. Cambridge Press, pp. 263-276.

www.ingramcontent.com/pod-product-compliance
Lightning Source LLC
Chambersburg PA
CBHW070929080526
44589CB00013B/1447